Good Morning Beautiful Child of God
A Modern Day Psalm of Hope & Love

Published by Diane Castillo White & Shannon Farrouge

Photography by Shannon Oberg

ISBN: 979-8-9860994-0-8

Library of Congress Control Number: 2024909965

Printed in the United States of America

Scripture quotations marked NIV are from:
THE HOLY BIBLE, NEW INTERNATIONAL VERSION®, NIV®
Copyright © 1973, 1978, 1984, 2011 by Biblica, Inc.®
Used by Permission of Biblica, Inc.® All rights reserved worldwide.

Scripture quotations marked ESV are from the ESV® Bible
(The Holy Bible, English Standard Version®), copyright © 2001 by Crossway,
a publishing ministry of Good News Publishers. Used by permission.

For information contact: hello@goodmorningbeautifulchildofgod.com

Good Morning Beautiful Child of God!

A Modern Day Psalm of Hope & Love

Diane Castillo White
Shannon Farrouge

Photography • Shannon Oberg

Preface

I went back to college in 2008 in an effort to finish my art degree. One day at school, I met with a young lady who was going through a sad season, struggling in her relationships with her father, boyfriend and God.

That night while sleeping, my soul was stirred with concern for her. I heard words that were spoken quickly and piercing with Holy Spirit wisdom. I leaped from the bed saying to myself, "I have to write this down!"

In awe and with much delight, I looked down at what was written and said, "Lord, you gave me an edited version of what I heard!"

The next time I saw the young lady, I gave her a copy of the poem and wrote at the top:

To: Her name _____
Love: Diane

I did not see her again and do not know what the poem meant to her, but I do know that the words I was given have helped me through many times of darkness and with my spiritual growth.

In the years that followed, I kept talking about how this poem should be turned into a book to help encourage others. My daughter believed in the vision to help others with these words and moved a little bit of heaven and earth to make this book happen.

As a mother, sister, auntie and grandma, I have often thought, "What if I only had one chance to share the hope and love of God to encourage someone in their navigation through this difficult journey of the heart?"

And this poem is just that, encouragement and wisdom for life's journey.

With the humble sweetness and talent of others it is finally here: Good Morning Beautiful Child of God!

Blessings and Peace to you,

Diane Castillo White

This book belongs

To:

Love:

As I wake up in the morning I tell myself...

I am alone.

"Never will I leave you; never will I forsake you."

Hebrews 13:5 NIV

What will I do today?

Who am I?

For we are God's handiwork, created in Christ Jesus to do good works, which God prepared in advance for us to do.

Ephesians 2:10 NIV

Why am
I here?

But you are a chosen race,
a royal priesthood, a holy nation,
a people for his own possession,
that you may proclaim the
excellencies of him who called
you out of darkness into
his marvelous light.

1 Peter 2:9 ESV

Will I

be happy today?

Will my father offer me an understanding word?

¹⁹ "Do not lay up for yourselves treasures on earth, where moth and rust destroy and where thieves break in and steal, ²⁰ but lay up for yourselves treasures in heaven, where neither moth nor rust destroys and where thieves do not break in and steal. ²¹ For where your treasure is, there your heart will be also."

Matthew 6:19-21 ESV

Will my boyfriend validate my existence by telling me I am beautiful and wise?

Am I now trying to win the approval
of human beings, or of God?
Or am I trying to please people?
If I were still trying to please people,
I would not be a servant of Christ.

Galatians 1:10 NIV

Look around and see despair... injustice... futility.

I care so I cry and I cry and I cry

"He will wipe every tear from their eyes. There will be no more death or mourning or crying or pain, for the old order of things has passed away."

Revelation 21:4 NIV

Then I remember I have a Heavenly Father who loves and accepts me

I shall not seek approval from men on earth

For God so loved the world that he gave his one and only Son, that whoever believes in him shall not perish but have eternal life.[17] For God did not send his Son into the world to condemn the world, but to save the world through him.

John 3:16-17 NIV

The Lord is my Father, the Son is my friend,

No longer do I call you servants, for the servant does not know what his master is doing; but I have called you friends, for all that I have heard from my Father I have made known to you.

John 15:15 ESV

I am also my friend.

The Father tells me all is permissible, but not all things are beneficial

¹⁵ See, I set before you today life and prosperity, death and destruction. ¹⁶ For I command you today to love the Lord your God, to walk in obedience to him, and to keep his commands, decrees and laws; then you will live and increase, and the Lord your God will bless you in the land you are entering to possess.

Deuteronomy 30:15-16 NIV

So when I awake

I will ask the Lord to renew my mind

Do not be conformed to this world, but be transformed by the renewal of your mind, that by testing you may discern what is the will of God, what is good and acceptable and perfect.

Romans 12:2 ESV

I will say to myself...

Good Morning Beautiful Child of God!

See what great love the Father has lavished on us, that we should be called children of God! And that is what we are!

1 John 3:1 NIV

Today I do not know what will bring,

Your kingdom come,
your will be done,
on earth as it is in heaven.

Matthew 6:10 ESV

So Lord, although
I care and cry,

Fear not, for I am with you;
be not dismayed, for I am your God;
I will strengthen you, I will help you,
I will uphold you with my righteous right hand.

Isaiah 41:10 ESV

my grief will pass

If we confess our sins, he is faithful and just and will forgive us our sins and purify us from all unrighteousness.

1 John 1:9 NIV

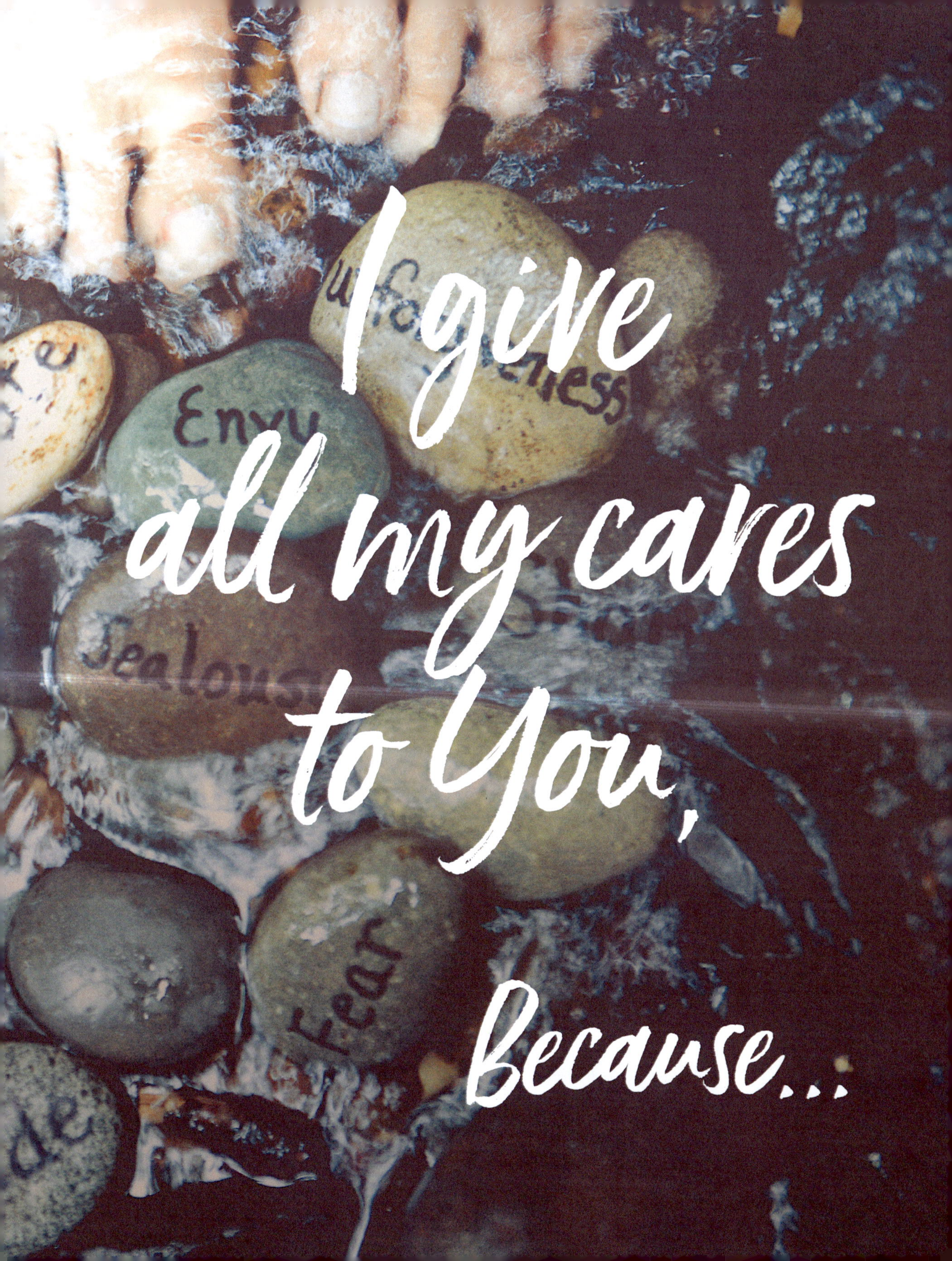
I give
all my cares
to You,
Because...
Envy
Fear

You Are!

I will praise you as long as I live, and in your name I will lift up my hands.

Psalm 63:4 NIV

Good Morning
Beautiful
Child of God!

As I wake up in the morning
I tell myself I am alone.
What will I do today? Who am I?
Why am I here? Will I be happy today?
Will my father offer me an understanding word?
Will my boyfriend validate my existence
by telling me I am beautiful and wise?
I look around and see despair, injustice, futility.
I care so I cry and I cry and I cry.
Then I remember
I have a Heavenly Father who loves and accepts me.
The Lord is my Father, the Son is my friend,
I am also my friend.
The Father tells me all is permissible
but not all things are beneficial.
So when I awake
I will ask the Lord to renew my mind.
I will say to myself
Good morning beautiful child of God!
Today I do not know what will bring, but
I know You my Father will be with me
and Your Will will be done!
So Lord, although I care and cry,
my grief will pass.
I give all my cares to You because
You Are!

Biographies

Shannon Farrouge &
Diane Castillo White

Diane Castillo White is an artist and potter living in the Pacific Northwest with her husband. She enjoys volunteering in her community and helping take care of her grandchildren and flowers. Her artistic focus is making creations that speak of God's beauty and presence in our daily lives.

Shannon Farrouge is a licensed professional counselor who has worked with thousands of women offering principles of hope and healing. She is currently creating group curriculum for the local church to help make essential counseling principles accessible for all.

Shannon Oberg is a traveling photographer and entrepreneur. Her life passion is to empower women to know their value and use their gifts to impact lives. She enjoys drinking coffee and creating space for people to rest at her farm in Maui.

Shannon Farrouge &
Shannon Oberg (photographer)

Notes

www.ingramcontent.com/pod-product-compliance
Lightning Source LLC
Chambersburg PA
CBRC090834120626
46547CB00009B/683